TIME'S REACH

JANET LORIMER

FEARON EDUCATION
Belmont, California

Simon & Schuster
Supplementary Education Group

The PACEMAKER BESTELLERS

Bestellers I

Diamonds in the Dirt
Night of the Kachina
The Verlaine Crossing
Silvabamba
The Money Game

Flight to Fear
The Time Trap
The Candy Man
Three Mile House
Dream of the Dead

Bestellers II

Black Beach
Crash Dive
Wind Over Stonehenge
Gypsy
Escape from Tomorrow

The Demeter Star
North to Oak Island
So Wild a Dream
Wet Fire
Tiger, Lion, Hawk

Bestellers III

Star Gold
Bad Moon
Jungle Jenny
Secret Spy
Little Big Top

The Animals
Counterfeit!
Night of Fire and Blood
Village of Vampires
I Died Here

Bestellers IV

Dares
Welcome to Skull Canyon
Blackbeard's Medal
Time's Reach
Trouble at Catskill Creek

The Cardiff Hill Mystery
Tomorrow's Child
Hong Kong Heat
Follow the Whales
A Changed Man

Cover and interior illustrator: Nanette Biers
Copyright © 1988 by Fearon Education, 500 Harbor Boulevard, Belmont, California 94002. All rights reserved. No part of this book may be reproduced by any means, transmitted, or translated into a machine language without written permission from the publisher.
ISBN 0-8224-5338-X

Library of Congress Catalog Card Number: 87-80128

Printed in the United States of America

1. 9 8 7 6 5 4 3 2

CONTENTS

1 ANDY 1
2 MAGGIE 7
3 COLIN 13
4 HOW DOES THIS WORK? 21
5 DOCTOR DALTON'S PAPERS 27
6 MONEY 33
7 NO ANSWERS 41
8 TIME 49
9 TRAVEL 59

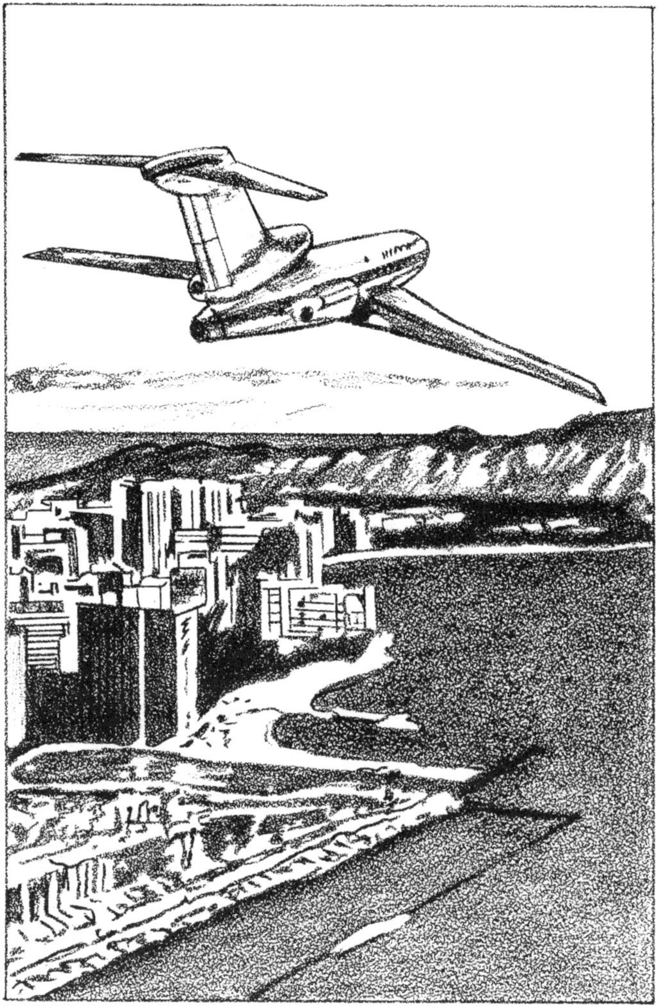

CHAPTER 1
ANDY

"We'll be landing in Honolulu soon, miss," the stewardess said. "Are you finished with your tea?"

Gail Crandall smiled and handed her empty cup to the stewardess. Then she turned to look out the window. She could hardly believe she was going to Hawaii. Soon she'd be starting a dream vacation with Andy.

Gail thought back to the call she'd gotten last week. What a surprise it had been. Her brother was the last person she'd expected to hear from.

Doctor Andrew Crandall was ten years older than Gail. When she started high school, he'd already become an archeologist. Gail didn't get to see her brother very often. Andy's work took him around the world. But when she graduated from college, she hoped Andy would be able to come home. She was really disappointed when he couldn't be there.

Then, after she graduated, Andy called from Hawaii. "Andy!" Gail had cried, "What are you doing in Hawaii?"

"It's a long story," he'd said. "How would you like to come visit me for a few weeks?"

"Like it? I'd love it!"

"Great! Start packing. I'll send you a plane ticket tomorrow. It's my present." Gail was so happy she could hardly speak. Hawaii and Andy. What a vacation it would be!

Gail saw Andy in the crowd as soon as she stepped off the plane. They hugged each other and then Andy stepped back.

"I want to take a look at you," he said. "I don't believe it! You're all grown up!"

Gail began to laugh, but she was thinking that Andy had changed, too.

They did look like sister and brother. Both had thick brown hair, gray eyes, and wide smiles.

Gail said, "Did you think I was still a child with braces on my teeth?"

"No," Andy said. "But I didn't know my little sister had become such a beautiful woman."

"Why, thank you!" Gail said. She was thinking that Andy looked a lot older. He had some gray in his hair and new lines in his face. She hoped he wasn't working too hard.

"Let's get your suitcases," Andy said. "Then we'll have a good talk on the way home."

While they waited for the suitcases, Gail looked around at the large crowd of people. Suddenly she saw a very good-looking young man staring at Andy. The stranger was tall and thin. He had dark hair and dark eyes. There was an ugly red cut in the shape of a U on one cheek. Gail knew it would leave a scar. She wondered how he had gotten hurt.

The man didn't take his eyes off Andy. Gail tapped her brother on the arm. "Do you know that man who's looking at you?" she asked.

Andy turned around. "No, I've never seen him before." Then he grinned. "But I don't think he was looking at me, Gail. I think he was looking at you."

"Was?" Gail turned and saw that the man was gone.

"I can see I'm going to have some problems while you're here," Andy said. "You'll have every young man in Honolulu knocking on my door!"

"Oh, Andy!" Gail said. She felt her face turn red. "Don't be silly!"

As soon as Andy got Gail's suitcases, they started walking to the parking lot. Andy was in front. Suddenly Gail saw the stranger again. He was watching Andy. Gail was sure of it this time. When the stranger saw that Gail was watching him, he turned and walked away.

As they left the airport, Gail said, "How far from here do you live?"

"About ten miles," Andy said. "It's near the Bishop Museum, where I work."

"You still haven't told me why you came to Hawaii," Gail said. "The last I heard you were in South America."

"Well, it all happened very suddenly. Does the name Doctor Willard Dalton ring a bell?"

"I don't think so. Should it?"

"I guess not. You were pretty young when I was in college. Doctor Dalton was one of my favorite teachers. After I graduated, we worked together and became good friends. Then five years ago, I had to go to South America. Doctor Dalton came to Hawaii. He found what was left of a very old Hawaiian village. It's on the island of Molokai. He and his workers found a lot of artifacts. There were tools, cooking pots, and many other things. The artifacts help us understand how the people lived then."

"That sounds interesting," Gail said. "So you came to Hawaii to help him?"

Andy shook his head. "Not till just recently. First I had to finish my job in South America.

"Doctor Dalton had run into one big problem. A builder wanted to put up new houses right where the village was. So Doctor Dalton and his workers had to hurry to dig up the artifacts. He sent boxes and boxes of them to the museum. Many of them are still in storage. Some are on display. It was taking years to sort through them all.

"Then, three weeks ago, Dr. Dalton got sick with the flu. He asked me to come to Hawaii to help him. I was able to come right away. But a few days after I got here, Dr. Dalton died."

CHAPTER **2**

MAGGIE

"Oh, Andy, I am sorry," Gail said. "What happened?"

"He had a heart attack," Andy said.

Gail didn't know what to say. She could tell how upset Andy was.

"By the way," Andy said. "I have to warn you about my house. It's not really ready for company. In fact, it's a mess. On top of that, Doctor Dalton gave me some papers to look at. They're the notes he made about the village. I think there are some pictures, too. I haven't had time to put them in order."

Gail laughed. "Is that why you wanted me to come to Hawaii? To clean up your house?"

"Of course not. You should know me better than that, Gail."

"It was just a joke," she said. "But I would like to help. Maybe I could sort out those papers. I'd be very careful with them."

Andy thought for a minute. "It would be a big help," he said. "But don't forget, you're on vacation."

"I know," Gail said. "I'm going to enjoy myself while I'm here. But I'm sure I can find some time to help you, too."

Andy parked in front of the small house he rented. It was in a yard full of beautiful trees and flowers. Andy explained that the weather was warm and wet. The plants seemed to take care of themselves.

They carried the suitcases into the house. The moment she walked in, Gail saw Andy's mess. It looked as if he'd been living out of suitcases the whole time he'd been there. Clothes and books and other things lay all over the place.

"I did warn you," Andy laughed.

He led Gail down the hall to a small bedroom. Boxes in the corners of the room made it seem very crowded. "These are Doctor Dalton's papers," Andy said.

"It looks like I'll have enough to keep me busy," Gail laughed.

Andy nodded. "I'm afraid so. I hardly have time to get my work done at the museum. In fact, I'm going to have to hire someone to help me. I'm looking for an archeology student who needs a summer job."

"Well, don't worry about me," Gail said. "I plan to spend a lot of time at the beach."

"Tomorrow I'm going to take the day off. Would you like to go sight-seeing?"

"Sounds great," Gail said.

Suddenly they heard a loud knock on the front door. Andy frowned. "I hope that's not someone from the museum," he said. "I told them I'd be taking today and tomorrow off."

Andy went to answer the door. When he opened it, Gail saw a small angry-looking woman. Before Andy could say anything, the woman walked into the room. "Okay, Doctor Crandall," she said. "I want those papers!"

"I didn't ask you to come in, Maggie Dalton."

"I don't care," she said. "And I won't leave until I get what I came for." She glared at Gail. "Who's this?"

"This is my sister, Gail," Andy said. "I warn you, Maggie, leave her out of this. She's here on vacation. I won't have you upsetting her." Then he turned to Gail. "Maggie is Doctor Dalton's daughter. She wants her father's papers. But she isn't going to get them. If she ever comes here while I'm out, just call the police."

"Knock it off, Doctor Crandall," Maggie sneered. "I'm not afraid of you. Those papers belonged to my father. Now they should belong to me. I *want* them!"

Andy shook his head. "No way, Maggie. We talked about it before. Your father told me to keep those papers out of your hands. Now get out of my house!"

Maggie turned and stamped out. Andy banged the door shut behind her.

"I don't get it," Gail said. "Why would she want those papers? Is she an archeologist, too?"

Andy laughed. "Maggie writes a gossip column. She says she wants to write a book about her father. But Doctor Dalton didn't trust her. I have no idea why she really wants those papers. I'll bet she thinks she can make some money from them. Money's about the only thing Maggie ever thinks of."

Gail frowned. "You said the papers had to do with what Doctor Dalton found in that village. It doesn't seem likely they could bring in all that much money. Wouldn't her father have told you if they were worth a lot?"

Andy shrugged. "Maggie's a strange person," he said. "Nobody I know understands her. But look, let's not talk about her anymore. I want to take you out to dinner."

While Gail got ready to go out, she thought about Maggie Dalton. Why did the woman want those papers? Gail decided to go through them soon.

Later, after they'd come back from dinner, Gail got ready for bed. Then she turned out the light and went to the window. There was a full moon. The air was sweet with the scent of flowers. A warm wind was blowing.

Suddenly Gail frowned. She thought she saw something move in the shadows across the street. Then she saw a man move out of the shadows. For a minute, he stood on the street corner, staring at the house. Then he turned and walked away. When he stepped under the streetlight, Gail saw him clearly. She gasped. It was the stranger who had been at the airport.

He must have followed them. But why?

While she was asking herself this question, she saw someone else in the shadows. When this person stepped into the light, Gail saw that it was Maggie Dalton. What was she doing there? Was she with the stranger? Was she following him? As Gail watched, Maggie moved after the man. She seemed to be following him.

Maggie wanted Doctor Dalton's papers. Was that what the stranger wanted, too?

CHAPTER **3**
COLIN

The next morning Andy woke Gail early. "We have a lot to do today," he told her. "I want to drive around the island and show you as much as I can. I thought we would take a lunch and eat at the beach. How does that sound?"

"Like a lot of fun," Gail said.

While she was getting dressed, Gail thought of what she'd seen the night before. Should she tell Andy? She decided she wouldn't. Not yet. Andy had enough to think about.

She and Andy had a wonderful day together. Andy took her to see the Pali Lookout. It was on a high mountain in the middle of the island. From there they could see for miles.

Then they went to Waikiki. This was the heart of Honolulu and a very busy part of the city. It was filled with tourists. There were lots of shops for Gail to enjoy. She bought postcards and a beautiful *lei*. The *lei* was made of black *kukui* nuts.

Andy told her that the Hawaiians who lived long ago had used the nuts for many things. "They burned the oil from the nuts in their stone lamps," he said. "They used the nuts for food. And they made the necklace we call a *lei*."

"I always thought a *lei* was made of flowers," Gail said.

"A *lei* can be made from flowers," Andy said. "It can also be made from nuts, seashells, and other things."

After they left Waikiki, Gail and Andy drove around the island. They stopped at one of the beach parks for lunch. Gail couldn't get over the beautiful sights. "Look at the colors of the water," she exclaimed. "Blue, green, and even purple!"

By the time they got home, Gail was tired but happy. "What a day!" she said. "I had so much fun."

"We'll do it again," Andy said as they climbed the front steps. "You know I—"

Andy was interrupted by a loud noise. He ran into the house with Gail right behind him.

Someone had broken in. The place looked even worse than it had when Gail had first seen it. "We must have surprised the robbers," Andy said. "That was the back door we heard."

"Call the police," Gail said.

"Hold on a minute. Let's first see if anything's missing. I've got a feeling nothing is. I don't own much that's worth stealing."

"What about Dr. Dalton's papers?" Gail asked. "Maybe Maggie did this."

Andy began to laugh. "Maggie may be hard to get along with. But I don't think she'd break the law. No, I think I know what happened. A lot of houses around here have been broken into. The robbers are looking for something they can sell. I bet they were pretty mad when they found out I don't even have a TV."

Andy searched the house, found nothing missing, and then called the police.

Gail remembered the stranger who'd been watching the house the night before. Had he broken in while they were out?

The next morning Andy got a call from the museum. He groaned after he hung up. "I have to go in for a few hours," he said. "I'd hoped to get more time off."

"That's okay," Gail said. "I want to go to the beach and lie in the sun."

"Good idea," Andy said. "Why don't you take my car? I can walk to the museum. In fact, it would be good for me. I spend too much time sitting behind a desk."

"I'll meet you back here for lunch," Gail said.

At the beach, it was very crowded. It took Gail a while to find a place to roll out her beach mat.

When she finally did, she looked more closely at the people nearby. And there, just a few feet away, sat the good-looking stranger. He was watching her. Suddenly Gail felt cold all over.

She looked around quickly. With so many people, she should be safe enough. The stranger wouldn't do anything to her in this crowded place. Or at least she hoped he wouldn't.

The man stood, picked up his mat, and walked over to her. "Mind if I sit down?" he asked.

"It's a free beach," Gail said coldly.

"My name is Colin Walker. I saw you at the airport the other day. I guess you're here on a visit."

"Have you been following me?" Gail asked in an angry voice.

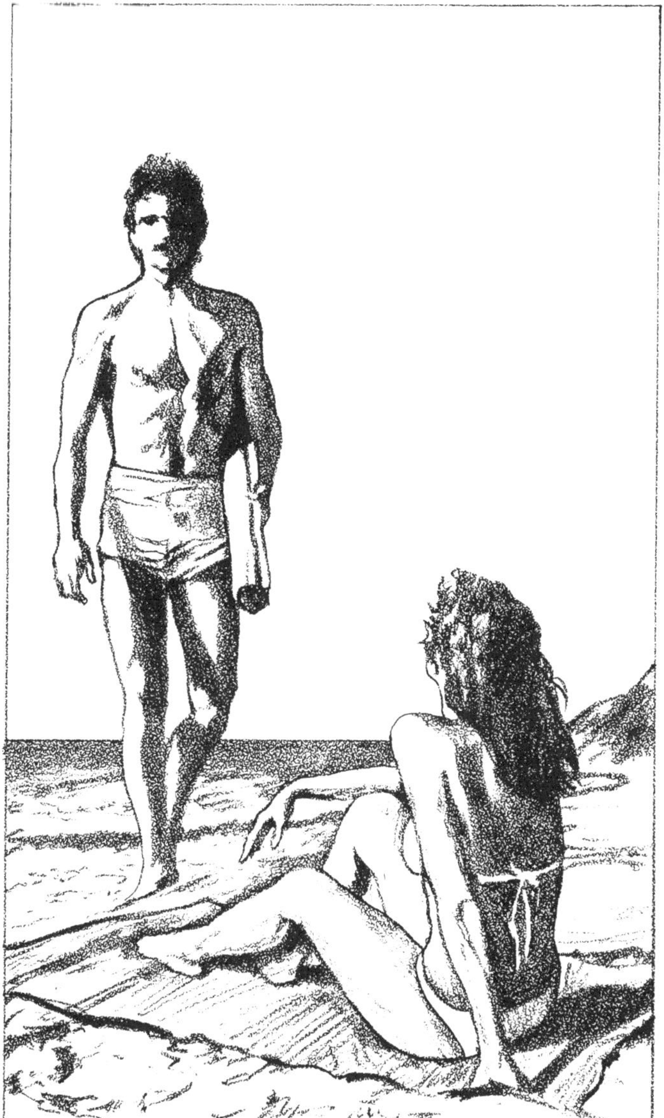

Colin Walker turned bright red. Gail thought he might try to lie. Instead he said, "Yes, I have. I guess you have a right to be angry. But I do have a good reason."

"Oh, sure," Gail sneered. "Sure you do."

"Please, don't be mad. Let me explain."

"Okay," Gail said. "Explain. But I warn you, this had better be good."

"It isn't you I wanted to meet," Colin said. "It's Doctor Crandall. You see, I heard he was looking for help. I really want to work in the museum. I study archeology at the university. I was hoping Doctor Crandall might hire me."

Gail frowned. "So why don't you go to the museum and *ask* my brother for a job. Why follow me?"

Colin hung his head. "I know, it sounds silly, but I did try once or twice. And each time I went to talk to him, I lost my nerve. I'm afraid he'll say no."

It did sound silly. But Gail thought she could understand Colin's problem. She, too, had felt frightened before asking for work.

"So why are you following me?" she asked.

"This will sound even sillier," he said. "I've been trying to work up my nerve to talk to

Doctor Crandall. The other day I was at the airport. I happened to see him meet your plane. I got an idea. I thought that maybe I could ask you to talk to him for me. I guess it doesn't make much sense, does it?"

Gail laughed. "Not much," she said. "You'll have to meet him and talk to him sometime."

"I know," Colin said, "but maybe you could put in a good word for me."

"I know nothing about you," Gail said.

"You know my name," Colin said. "And that's more than I know about you!"

CHAPTER **4**
HOW DOES THIS WORK?

Gail grinned. The man was something else. She wondered if his story were just a way of getting close to her. Or was there another reason? Was he after the papers?

Well, two could play the same game. She'd have to be careful, but she wanted to find out more about him.

"I'm Gail Crandall," she said. "I guess I could talk to Andy. I can tell him you're looking for a job. Maybe I can set it up so you two can meet. But that's all I can do."

"It would be a big help, Gail. Thank you."

"By the way," Gail said, "why were you watching Andy's house the other night?"

The question took Colin by surprise. "Wh- what do you mean?"

"Come off it," Gail said. "You were standing across the street. It was very late. I saw you!"

Colin hung his head. "You're right," he said. "I was watching the house. You see, I'd knocked on the door two hours before. I'd made up my mind I just had to talk to your brother. But no one was home. So I waited across the street. By the time you got home, it was too late. I guess I lost my nerve again."

"Did you?" Gail said. "Well, someone broke into the house yesterday. You wouldn't happen to know anything about it, would you?"

Colin looked shocked. "Gail, I didn't do that! In fact, I was helping my landlady all day. She needed some yard work done. She could tell you where I was yesterday."

Gail stared at Colin. It wouldn't be hard to check his story. But if he were telling the truth, who had broken in?

"Do you know a woman named Maggie Dalton?" Gail asked.

Colin looked away. "N-no, I don't think so," he said.

Gail was sure he was lying. Suddenly Colin jumped up. "Let's go for a swim," he said.

Gail followed him to the water. For the rest of the morning they went swimming or lay in the sun and talked. Gail found that she enjoyed his company. He was really very nice.

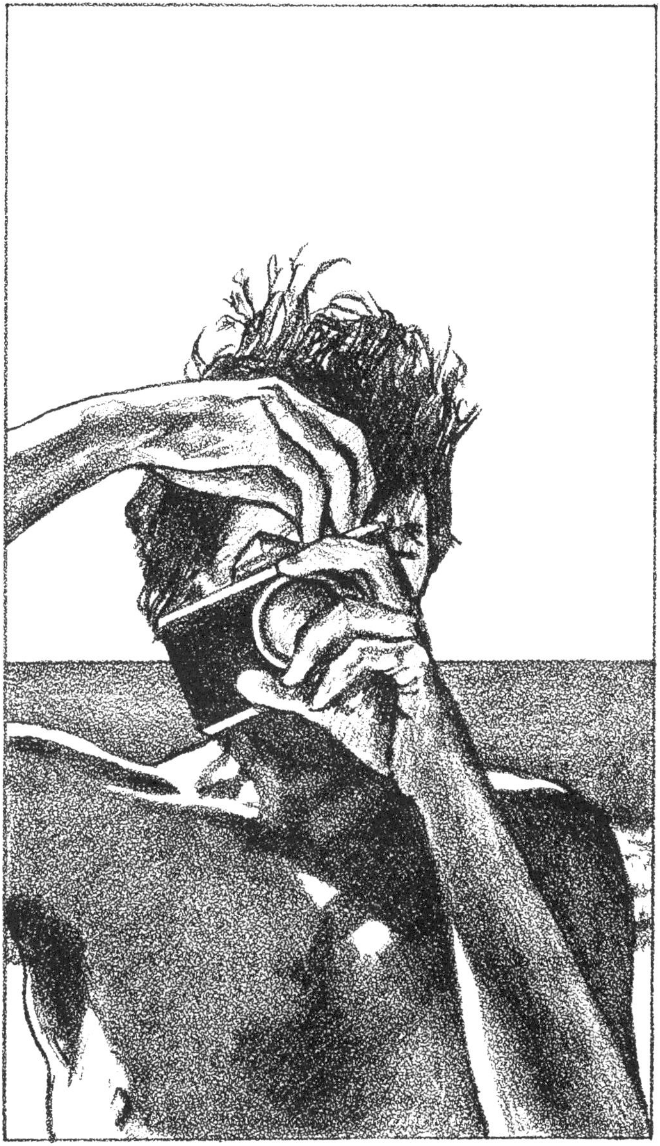

"Are you enjoying your visit?" Colin asked. "Have you done any sight-seeing?"

Gail told him about the trip she and Andy had made the day before. "I took a lot of pictures to show people at home. In fact, I think I'll take some more right now." She pulled her camera out of her beach bag. "Would you mind taking my picture?" she asked. "I want to show my friends that I really was on Waikiki Beach."

"Sure!" Colin took the camera. But then he frowned and said, "How does this thing work?"

Gail showed him. Colin acted as if he'd never seen a camera like Gail's before. And it wasn't a fancy camera.

After Colin took Gail's picture, she asked if she could take his. Colin said, "No, I wish you wouldn't."

"Why not?"

Colin put his hand up to his cheek. "I know how ugly this cut looks," he said. "I hate looking like this."

Gail shrugged. "Okay, if that's how you feel about it. But it doesn't look as bad as you think it does."

Colin looked at his watch. "It's noon," he said. "No wonder I'm hungry. Will you let me buy you some lunch?"

"Lunch!" Gail said. "I forgot! I'm supposed to meet Andy for lunch."

Colin looked disappointed. "I'm sorry you have to go."

"Well, you know the old saying," Gail laughed as she rolled up her beach mat. "Time sure flies when you're having fun."

Colin stared at Gail as if he didn't know what she was talking about. "You know," Gail said, "I mean that—"

"Oh, yes, I know what you mean. I guess I just never heard it put that way before."

Gail stared at him. She thought everyone had heard that saying. "I'm sorry I can't stay, Colin. This has been a lot of fun. What about tomorrow? Are you going to be busy?"

"No," he said with a bright smile. "I'd like to see you again. Tomorrow would be fine."

"Here," Gail said. "I'll give you my number. Why don't you call me in the morning? Then we can plan our day." She handed him a piece of paper. "By the way, do you have a car? Or can I give you a lift?"

"A what?" Colin asked.

"A lift. Can I give you a ride home?"

"Oh!" His face cleared. "No, thanks. I think I'll stay at the beach for a while."

"Okay," Gail said. As she walked to her car, she thought how strange Colin Walker was. Why didn't he understand some of the things she'd said? Why didn't he know how to work a camera?

At the same time, Gail liked him. Colin was nice and good-looking and fun to be with. There were a lot of things about him that made no sense. Still, Gail knew how she felt.

CHAPTER **5**
DOCTOR DALTON'S PAPERS

When Gail got home, Andy was making her lunch. While he cooked, she told him about meeting Colin. Andy frowned. "I'm not sure I like this man following you around," he said.

"Don't *worry*. I told you, he just wants to talk to you about that job."

"Are you going to see him again?" Andy asked.

"Sure. Why not?"

"You don't know anything about him."

Gail laughed. "Andy, give me a break. I'm a grown woman, remember? I can think for myself. And you're my brother, not my father."

"I have to take care of you," Andy said.

"Andrew, I can take care of myself."

After lunch Andy had to go back to the museum. "Things are really piled up there," he said.

"That's okay," Gail said. "It will give me time to go through Dr. Dalton's papers."

After Andy left, Gail brought out the boxes to the front room. When she opened them, she found many pages of notes. She also found a lot of pictures. She put the pictures in a pile to look at later.

Gail had been a little afraid that the notes wouldn't make sense to her. She'd also thought they might make very dull reading. Doctor Dalton's handwriting was hard to follow. But the notes were very interesting.

Soon Gail came across something that made her stop. She read the page again. Dr. Dalton had found something that should never have been in that village. It was a small machine that looked like a tiny computer. It was made of a metal the doctor knew nothing about. He'd found it with other artifacts, like stone lamps and tools. It had been in the ground for a long time.

But the doctor's find made no sense at all. The Hawaiians had never had anything like it. Nor, in fact, did the doctor know of *anyone* who had anything just like it. Not now or at any other time. Gail kept reading. She hoped to learn more about the strange machine. But Dr. Dalton wrote nothing else about it. Gail began to grow tired. She put the papers down and rubbed her eyes. Maybe she should stop for the day. But she didn't really want to. She decided to look at the pictures instead.

The pictures were just as interesting as the papers. They'd all been taken in the village. Most were of the artifacts and the workers.

Suddenly Gail frowned. There was a red circle around one man's face. Why would this picture have been marked? She looked carefully at the face. It looked like someone she knew. Then Gail gasped. It was Colin Walker! And on his cheek was the same cut Gail had seen that morning.

Gail rubbed her eyes again. She thought she had to be seeing things. But when she looked at the picture again, nothing had changed. That same cut was still on Colin's cheek. Gail turned the picture over. There was a date written on the back. The picture had been taken five years ago.

It just wasn't possible! The cut on Colin's cheek should have healed a long time ago. It should be only a scar by now. But Colin still had the same cut today that he had had five years ago.

Gail stared at the picture, trying to understand it. She couldn't. Then she had an idea. Maybe Doctor Dalton had written about it in his notes. She went through them again. She was looking for a page with the same date as the picture. In a while she found it.

Doctor Dalton had written that he'd caught Colin going through his things. He thought Colin was looking for something to steal. But before the doctor could question him, Colin got away.

Dr. Dalton couldn't find him. Later, when he saw that Colin was in one of the pictures he'd taken, he marked it. He didn't want to forget that young man.

Gail stared at the page. She knew she should tell Andy about this. But she didn't want to do that just yet. First she wanted to find out for herself what Colin was up to.

When Andy got home, Gail had put the papers back in the box. "How was your afternoon?" he asked.

"Oh, fine," Gail said. "I started to sort out Doctor Dalton's papers."

"Find anything interesting?"

"It was all interesting," Gail said. "I liked reading about the things he found in the village. How did the day go for you?"

"Not bad. But I'm afraid I have to work again tomorrow. I'm sorry, Gail. I really hoped I could get more time off to show you around."

"That's okay," she said. "I'm sure I can find something to do."

"Are you still planning on seeing that young man again?"

"Colin Walker? Look, big brother, I'm not about to get married. This is just a date!"

Andy smiled. "Okay, I get the point. I guess I'm coming on a bit strong, aren't I?"

Gail nodded. "If you ever want a new job," she joked, "you could always get one as a watchdog!"

"Thanks a lot!"

CHAPTER **6**
MONEY

When Colin called the next morning, Gail told him Andy had to work. "So I have the whole day free. I'd like to spend it with you, Colin. Shall I pick you up?"

"No!" he said quickly. "I'll meet you where we met yesterday."

Gail wondered if Colin didn't want her to know where he lived. But that didn't make much sense. Yesterday he'd used his landlady as his alibi for the day of the break-in. He would have known that Gail might check that alibi.

As soon as Colin hung up, Gail called the telephone operator. She asked for Colin's number and address. The operator told her the number wasn't listed.

Gail met Colin at the beach. They had a great time together. But Gail soon found it was hard to get Colin to talk about himself. When she'd ask him a personal question, he'd change the subject.

Colin did know a lot about archeology. It was interesting to hear him talk about it. The more time Gail spent with Colin, the more she liked him.

At noon, Colin asked Gail if he could buy her lunch.

"Why, thank you," she said. "That would be nice. How about hot dogs? There's a stand over—" Then she saw the look on his face.

"Hot dogs?" he asked slowly.

Gail stared at him. It was almost as if he didn't know what a hot dog was.

"Yes, you know—"

"Oh, hot dogs!" Colin grinned. "Sure, let's get a hot dog."

They walked to the hot dog stand. Colin made small talk on the way. Gail didn't listen very closely. She was thinking about Colin and the things he didn't seem to know about.

After lunch, she asked him if he'd like to meet Andy. "We can drive over to the museum right now," she said. "I told him you were looking for a job. He said he'd like to talk to you."

Colin looked surprised. "Right now?" he asked. "I'm covered with sand. I'd like to clean up first and—"

"Oh, come on!" Gail laughed. "Andy won't care. He knows I planned to meet you at the beach. Don't worry. I'll tell him it was my idea."

When they got to the museum, Gail asked where Andy's office was. Andy had told them his sister was in town and might be dropping by. Everyone at the museum seemed more than happy to meet her and help her. Gail and Colin had no trouble getting in to see him.

When Andy and Colin met, Gail had to hide a smile. Andy looked Colin up and down very carefully. His look seemed to say, "So you're the man who's so interested in my sister!" Poor Andy! He couldn't help himself.

"I think I'll take a look around the museum," Gail said. "You two can get to know each other."

"Good idea," Andy said. "There's a lot to see, Gail, so take your time."

The museum was larger than Gail had thought it would be. She saw some of the artifacts that Doctor Dalton had brought back from Molokai. Yesterday she'd seen pictures. Now she was seeing the real things. She wondered where

36 *Time's Reach*

the rest of the artifacts were. Then she remembered that Doctor Dalton had not had time to study them all. Some were still packed away in the storeroom.

Suddenly Gail felt a tap on her arm. She turned and saw Maggie Dalton standing behind her.

"I want to talk to you," Maggie said.

"What are you doing here?" Gail asked.

"I've been trying to get in to see your brother. I have to talk to him about those papers."

"Forget it! Andy made it clear to you the other day. He's not going to give them to you."

Maggie glared at Gail. Then she said, "Look, we have to talk."

"We don't have anything to talk about," Gail said coldly. She started to walk away but Maggie came after her.

"Oh, I think there's lots to talk about, Gail. Why don't we start with Colin Walker?"

Gail stopped and turned to face Maggie. "What about him?"

Maggie grinned. "I thought that would interest you." Then she looked around. "We can't talk here. Let's go outside. I don't want anyone to hear us."

Outside they found a cool spot on the grass under a big tree. After they sat down, Maggie said, "I want to know if you've read my father's papers."

"Why would I do that?" Gail asked. "I'm not an archeologist."

"Listen," Maggie said. "I've seen you at the beach with Colin Walker. You do want to know what's going on, don't you?"

"What does Colin Walker have to do with your father's papers?"

"Okay, Gail, I'm going to tell you everything I know. I want you to understand why I need those papers."

Maggie looked around to make sure no one was listening. "Andy probably told you about the village my father came across five years ago. I think my father found something valuable there. I think Colin knows what it is and wants to get it. I also think my father wrote about it in his notes."

"What do you think your father found?"

Maggie shook her head. "I don't know, but I'm sure it's worth a lot."

"Maybe you're wrong," Gail said. "Maybe he found the kinds of things people have seen many times before."

"No, no! My father told me it was worth a lot of money."

"How can you be so sure? You don't even know what it is."

"I'll tell you," Maggie said. "My father got sick with the flu. I went to his house to see how he was doing. We didn't get along very well. But he was my father, and he was sick. When I got close to the house, I saw Colin run out the front door. I didn't know who he was then. But

I wondered why he was running so fast. I went into the house and I found my father out of bed. He was very upset. He said something about a priceless discovery."

Maggie's eyes were bright. "Did you hear me, Gail? A *priceless* discovery!"

Gail nodded. "Go on," she said.

"Then my father tried to say something else, but he started gasping. Colin had upset him so much he had a heart attack. I don't know what Colin said. But I think he knew what my father had found. I think he was trying to get his hands on it."

All of a sudden, Gail stopped listening to Maggie. She knew what had upset Doctor Dalton. It wasn't what Colin had said. It was the cut on Colin's cheek—a new cut that was five years old.

CHAPTER **7**
NO ANSWERS

"Maggie," Gail said, "you have to tell me what your father said to you before he died. It could be the answer."

Maggie frowned. "So far I'm doing all the talking."

"Believe me," Gail said, "I don't know anything. But maybe I can help you. Maybe I can get Colin to talk."

"Okay. . . . Just before my father died, he said, 'I didn't understand! I didn't know what I'd found! What a priceless discovery. I was wrong to hide it from him. Tell him—' Then my father gasped. His last words made no sense to me. He cried out, *'Kukui!* Tell Colin . . . *kukui!'* "

Gail frowned. Maggie was right. Doctor Dalton's words made no sense. Then Gail remembered the day she had bought the *lei*. Andy had told her what the Hawaiians had used the *kukui* nuts for. Gail wished she could remember more of what he'd said.

"You see?" Maggie said. "My father found something worth a lot of money. I don't know what it is. But I figured that a good place to start looking was in those papers."

Maggie Dalton made Gail feel sick. All the woman cared about was money. Gail didn't want to have anything to do with her.

Colin, however, did seem to have some kind of problem. Gail didn't know what it was. But she would do what she could to help him.

"Now tell me about those papers," Maggie said. "Have you read them?"

"I started to," Gail said. "But I haven't finished yet."

Maggie glared at Gail. "I warn you, don't hold out on me! I'm going to keep an eye on you. If you try anything funny, you'll be sorry."

Gail stood up. "And I told you, I haven't finished reading the papers. You'll just have to believe me, Maggie."

Maggie looked very angry. "Why should I trust you?"

"Because I'm the only one who can help you."

"Oh, all right," Maggie said. "Look, try to get Colin to talk to you. Find out what he knows. And by the way, be careful. Colin isn't what he says he is."

"What do you mean?" Gail asked.

"I did some checking. He's not a student at the university."

"Oh? Well, do you know where he lives?"

Maggie nodded. "He's renting a guesthouse a few blocks from here. I'll give you his address and telephone number. He seems to like you a lot, Gail. Use that! Use *him!* Just find that thing and we'll both be rich!"

"I have to get back now," Gail said. "Andy will be wondering what happened to me." She took the paper with Colin's telephone number and address. She started to walk away. Maggie grabbed her arm.

"Remember," Maggie said between gritted teeth, "don't try anything on your own. If you hold out on me—"

Gail shook her arm free. "Knock it off, Maggie!"

"I'll call you tomorrow," Maggie said. "By then, you can finish reading those papers!"

That night at dinner, Andy told Gail that he planned to hire Colin. She stared at him in surprise. "I thought you didn't like him," she said.

"It wasn't *him* I didn't like. What I didn't like was his following you around."

Gail grinned. "I see. Well, what made you decide to hire him?"

"He knows a lot about archeology. He talks like someone who's been working at it for a while. He's a very interesting young man."

Maggie had said that Colin wasn't a student. If he were an archeologist, why had he lied? Gail had lots of questions but no answers. There had to be a way to find out what was going on. And then Gail began to get a wild idea. Just thinking about it made her afraid.

"By the way," Andy said, breaking into her thoughts, "about tomorrow. I'm afraid I have some bad news. You see—"

"Don't tell me. Let me guess. You have to work again."

"I'm afraid so," Andy said. "Look. Maybe in a few days—"

"It's all right," Gail laughed. "I understand. You have to make a living, right? I'm the one on vacation. Besides, I was thinking of doing some shopping tomorrow. I need some new clothes for this hot weather."

In the morning, after Andy had left, Gail grabbed the car keys and the map. She found Colin's street and parked up the block from his house. Then she found a store with a telephone.

When Colin answered the phone, Gail said quickly, "It's me. Are you free today? Can we get together?"

Colin didn't say anything for a moment. Gail hoped nothing was wrong. Then Colin said, "Sure. I don't have any plans. Where would you like to meet?"

"How about the zoo?" Gail said. "Andy and I drove by it the other day."

"Okay," Colin said. "I can catch the bus and meet you there in an hour."

"That's fine," Gail said.

Gail bought a soft drink and waited in the store. She watched Colin's house. Soon she saw him. He walked down the street to the bus stop. As soon as he was out of sight, Gail ran across the street.

When she rang the bell on the front door, Colin's landlady answered it. "I'm looking for Colin Walker," Gail said. "I understand he lives here."

"He rents the guesthouse in back," the woman said. "I don't know if he's home or not. I don't keep track of what he does. You can go see for yourself. Look, my favorite TV show is on, so . . ."

Gail nodded. "Sorry!" she said.

She ran to the backyard and found a small guesthouse. Gail looked around quickly, but no one seemed to be watching her. She found the door was locked. Her heart was beating fast.

Gail walked to the back of the guesthouse. She was in luck. Colin had left a window unlocked. In no time Gail climbed through it.

Gail didn't know where to start. She wasn't sure what she was looking for. She needed to find something that would tell her more about Colin.

He didn't own very much. Gail found some books and clothes. She was almost ready to give up when she opened the closet. In the back of the closet was a small machine. It looked very strange. It wasn't like anything Gail had ever seen before. She looked at it for several minutes. Then she decided to pull it out of the closet for a closer look. To her surprise, it was not at all heavy. But the moment she picked it up, lights went on. The machine made a loud noise. Gail jumped back, almost dropping the thing. She put it down quickly. What in the world was it? How could she turn it off?

While she was trying to turn it off, the door suddenly banged open. Gail cried out in surprise. Colin was standing there, and he looked very angry.

CHAPTER **8**
TIME

Gail couldn't move. She just stared at Colin. She didn't know what to do or say. She'd been caught, and there was no way out.

Suddenly Colin groaned. He went over to the bed and sat down. He put his head in his hands. "What a mess," he said. "I should have known it was hopeless."

Gail watched him in surprise. What had come over him? A minute ago Colin had looked so angry. Now he just seemed tired and sad. Gail knew that she could run out the door and never come back. But if she did, she wouldn't find out the truth about Colin. She walked over to the bed and sat down beside him.

"How did you know I'd be here?" she asked.

"I never gave you my number and address. And they're not listed. Where did you get them? From Maggie Dalton?"

"Yes," Gail said. "So you know her."

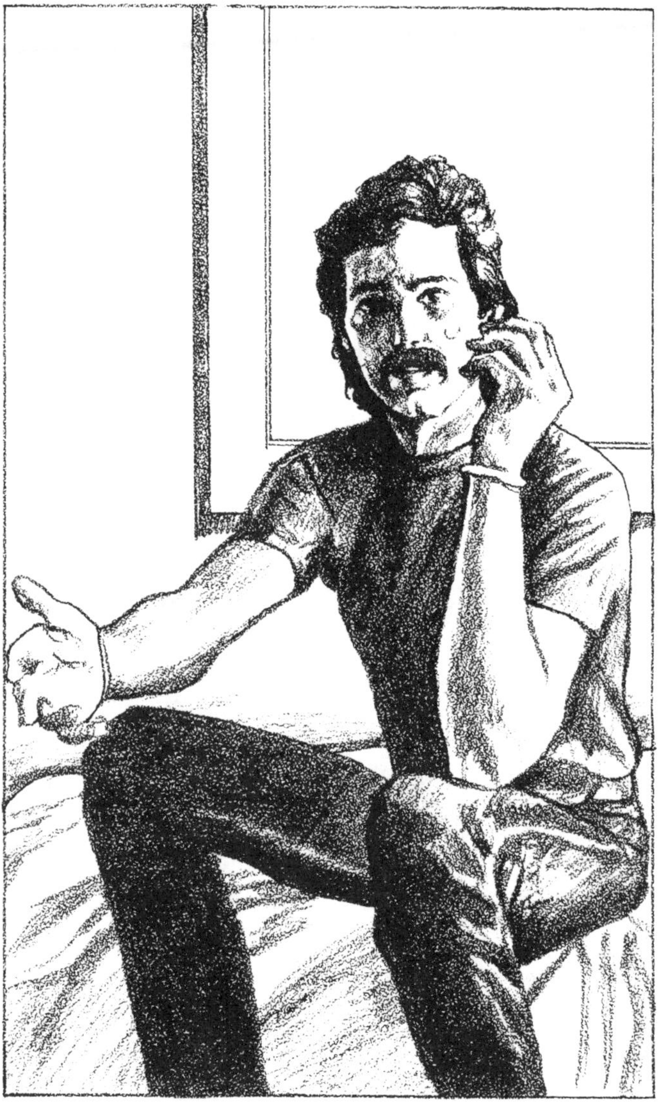

"I'm afraid so," Colin said.

"Maggie told me you were looking for something," Gail said. "She thinks it's something her father found on Molokai. Something worth a lot of money. She wants to find it so she can become rich. Is she right, Colin?"

Colin looked at her. He didn't look happy. "What about you, Gail? Are you out to get rich, too?"

"You didn't answer my question," Gail said.

Colin sighed. "I don't know what to say. I don't know who to trust. Look, Gail, Maggie is right in a way. I am looking for something. But it's not something I would sell. Besides, it was mine in the first place!"

Gail shook her head. "I'm not following you at all, Colin."

"I'll tell you what," Colin said. "If you tell me what you already know, I'll explain the rest of it. Fair enough?"

Gail nodded. She told Colin about Doctor Dalton's notes. She told him about the picture with the red circle around his face. She told him everything Maggie had said.

When Gail was finished, Colin said, "You know more than I thought you did."

"So I was right, wasn't I?" Gail said. "You do have a problem. You do need help. Why don't you tell me the truth?"

"The truth will surprise you," Colin said. "You may not want to believe it."

"Try me," Gail said.

Colin took both Gail's hands in his. He looked into her eyes. "I think you may have already come close to guessing the answer."

"What?"

"I'm . . . not one of you, Gail,"

"Wait a second, Colin."

"Oh, I'm human all right. I'm not from another planet or anything. I'm . . . from another time, Gail. I'm a time traveler. I come from the future."

"What?!"

"I know it's hard to believe, but it's true."

Gail stared at Colin. What he said seemed impossible. But it would explain some things. Like why Colin didn't know how to work her camera. And why he didn't seem to understand some of the things she'd said to him. "How often do you do this?" she asked.

He grinned. "As a matter of fact, I'm still learning how to do it right. This is only my second trip into your time. I've made a lot of mistakes, but I'm learning. Sometimes the hard way!"

Gail couldn't help laughing. "Maybe you should start at the beginning," she said. "I have a lot of questions!"

"Okay," Colin said. "Well, to begin with, I'm not a student. I said that because I wanted to get a job in the museum. I think the thing I'm looking for may be hidden there."

"And what are you looking for?"

Colin shook his head. "We're getting ahead of the story. Hold off on the questions for a bit, okay?"

Gail nodded. But she thought to herself, "Colin, you're too much. And I can't help it. I really do like you."

"I'm an archeologist," Colin said. "Just like your brother. In the future, we have time travel. Not everyone can use it, just some of us. People who need to know about the past. I was picked to travel back in time to old Hawaii. I wanted to study how the people lived then.

"On my first trip into the past, I visited that village on Molokai. I got close enough to watch people cooking and fishing and making tools. I saw children playing games. But I ran into trouble when I got too close. The people weren't supposed to see me. They spotted me and they were afraid. Some of them came after me with spears! I turned to run, and I fell. That's how I cut my cheek."

Gail's eyes grew wider.

"At the same time, I dropped something. It was what Doctor Dalton later found and what Maggie now wants."

"What is it?" Gail asked.

"A computer," Colin said.

"A computer? What's the big deal? We've got lots of computers."

"Not like this one you don't. This one's different from today's computers. For one thing, it's made of a metal no one knows about yet. Also, it stores and analyzes information about nearly everything I find. The air and water, the plants, animals, and humans. It finds answers to questions today's scientists haven't even thought of asking. And it's small enough to fit in a shirt pocket."

"And that's what you're trying so hard to find," Gail said. "That computer."

"That's right," Colin said. "The rules of time travel say you can't leave anything behind. You have to leave a place just the way you found it. I broke the rules when I dropped the computer."

"What did you do after you dropped it?"

"I ran to my time travel machine," Colin said, pointing to the small machine on the floor. "I didn't want a spear in my back. I went to my own time as fast as I could. That's when I found out I'd dropped the computer. I knew I had to get it. But I was afraid to go back to the same time. So I checked my history books. I learned that Doctor Dalton had found the village hundreds of years later. I thought that would be a much safer time to try again."

"What happened?" Gail asked.

"The second time I went back, five years ago, I was too late. I got to the village after Doctor Dalton had dug up the computer. He'd already hidden it. I acted like one of the workers so I could nose around the place. I went through his papers, but they didn't say where it was. Just before Dr. Dalton walked in on me, I saw a picture of myself. But then the doctor caught me, and I took off."

Gail couldn't help smiling. "You did mess things up, didn't you?"

"I said I was from the future. I didn't say I was smarter than anyone else."

Gail laughed. "Okay. What happened next?"

"I returned once more to my own time. But I knew I had to go back yet again. I picked a day that would be five years later. All this tripping around in time only took me a few hours."

"I'm beginning to understand," Gail said. "Go on."

"I decided I had to talk to Doctor Dalton and tell him the truth. I didn't want to, but it was the only way to get my computer. Doctor Dalton wasn't at the museum. He was at home, sick with the flu. I went to his house. The moment he saw me and the cut on my cheek, he remembered me! But he couldn't understand how I could still have the same cut. When I told him everything about myself, he got very excited. He wanted to help me. He was just about to tell me where the computer was hidden. Then we saw Maggie coming up the front walk. Doctor Dalton got very upset. He said Maggie must never find out about me. He said she was a nosy woman and he didn't trust her. He told me to leave at once and to come back later."

"So you ran out of the house," Gail said.

Colin nodded. "I panicked! I didn't stop to think. I just ran."

"Then Doctor Dalton had a heart attack," Gail said.

"Yes, I found that out later. I felt so bad. I didn't mean to upset him that much."

"You couldn't have known he'd have a heart attack," Gail said. "What did you do then?"

"I decided to stay put until I could get the computer. I began following your brother. He'd been a friend of Doctor Dalton's, and he worked in the museum. I thought he might lead me to it."

"Did you break into our house?" Gail asked.

Colin shook his head. "That must have been Maggie."

"We have to get the computer before she does," Gail said. "And maybe that won't be too hard."

Gail told Colin what Doctor Dalton had said to Maggie just before he died. "Does that mean anything to you?" she asked.

Colin frowned. "The word *kukui* means many things. I wonder . . . Wait a minute. Of course! Lamps! *Kukui* is also the Hawaiian word for lamp. Do you think—?"

"Those stone lamps Doctor Dalton found in the village!" Gail said. "I saw one in the museum yesterday!"

"The computer would just fit inside it," Colin said.

"It must be in one of the lamps in the storeroom," Gail said. "Not all the artifacts have been checked over yet. Come on, Colin."

CHAPTER **9**
TRAVEL

At the museum, Gail was surprised at how easy it was to get into the storeroom. The people who worked there were busy. They'd seen Gail and Colin before and they did not stop them.

It was a big room with no windows. There were boxes of artifacts piled in every corner. In the middle of the room was a long table.

Doctor Dalton had written on each box what was inside it. They had no trouble finding the right one. The lamps had been packed in paper. Colin took each one out and put it on the table. Two of the lamps were empty. The third one held what they were looking for.

"At last," Colin sighed. He lifted out the tiny computer. "I never thought I'd see it again!"

"Let's get everything put away," Gail said. "And then get out of here before someone catches on to us."

When they left the museum, Gail spotted Maggie's car. "Oh, no!" she groaned. "That woman is following us! Now what do we do?"

"We have to go back to my house," Colin said. "That's where my time travel machine is. And then—"

"Don't say it."

Colin picked up the time travel machine. He turned to Gail. "I'm afraid this is it," he said softly.

Gail didn't want to say good-bye. She wished Colin could stay or that she could go with him.

"I guess I'll never see you again," she whispered.

"Gail," Colin said. "I don't want to leave. But I have to. This is just the wrong time for us."

"Will there ever be a right time?" Gail asked.

Colin pushed some buttons on the machine.

He looked into Gail's eyes.

"Perhaps," he said. "Perhaps."

In a moment he was gone.